FRANCOFILAMENTS

Eileen G'Sell is an American poet and film critic with recent contributions to *Poetry, Oversound, Hyperallergic, Harp and Altar, The Chronicle of Higher Education, Jacobin, The Baffler, The Art Newspaper, The Los Angeles Review of Books,* and *The Hopkins Review*. Her first volume of poetry, *Life After Rugby,* was published by Gold Wake Press in 2018. In 2023, she received the Rabkin Prize for arts journalism. Her first book of nonfiction, *Lipstick*, will join Bloomsbury's Object Lessons series in 2025. She teaches writing and media studies at Washington University in St. Louis.

PRAISE for *Francofilaments*

Like an array of confections in a patisserie window, the beguilingly vibrant, compact poems in G'Sell's *Francofilaments* are as meticulously constructed as they are full of surprises. What appear at first like the breezy escapades of a playgirl *flâneuse* quickly reveal layers of complication and conflict embedded in the artifice, reminding us that chic derives from the German for 'skill,' glamour has roots in occult practice, and any pretty little thing might harbor 'more Annabel Lee than Lady Dior' at heart. But just as 'escapism, however tenuous, proves / the only recourse to agency,' it's by means of G'Sell's exquisite, signature spellwork on the page—her own 'gold // beaded swagger, velvet strut'—and the sheer aplomb with which she handles every turn (of phrase, of thought, and of line) that the poet comes to perform, and thereby possess, 'who she is / till she's nobody else.'
    — Timothy Donnelly

Francofilaments traces the intersecting webs of Francophilia, feminism and film with delicate precision and humor: 'I tread, bragging about how close I was / to ghosting all the Frenchmen and Frenching / all the ghosts'. G'Sell's poems blend pirouetting wordplay, frank address and invention in a way that is unexpected and illuminating.
    — Matthea Harvey

Glorious in its swagger and seduction, *Francofilaments* invited me to reimagine who I could be in this world once again as a woman and a poet—hop a plane back to Paris, be a *flâneuse*, to say 'I've gone fugitive too,' to be reckless again, obstinate in the pursuit of pleasure, to claim for myself the moment of the poem when 'The cathedral meets my gaze, and says, 'you are my cathedral." I want to walk the boulevards with the woman, all the women, in these poems, but also to *be* her, a woman who 'straddles, stuns, and smirks at the world', a little bit of Jean Seberg, Claire Danes, Agnès Varda—dare I say a little bit of Tina Turner, even, with her 'gold/beaded swagger, velvet strut eye full/ of bicep flexed for the sky'. Here are poems so full of mischief, wit, intelligence, and the snap of her indefatigable self. G'Sell offers the reader so many ways to create and discover a home within oneself. I came away wanting it all.
    — Heather Derr-Smith

Reading *Francofilaments* was like being swept through the streets of Paris at night, the clack of your interloper's heels matching the precision of her thought. Nonchalant, philosophical, and painfully comical, she observes French film in the same breath as household objects, as casual and haphazard as sex. Once, she didn't off herself because she got a ticket to Isabelle Huppert. We are all glad for it.
    — Laura Broadbent

The hard gloss of a ballet studio mirror and mirrorlike museum glass: light, luxury, longing, surfaces, glimpses, and glints. Against the curated, heightened backdrop of French cinema, in *Francofilaments* the self, smudged, relishes and yearns. Here poems are rooms with tousled sheets, poems sharpened with rouge, crimson, and cerise, dense with sounds dropping and sliding and tangling together. The poems in this book are like an afternoon so beautiful it hurts, like the acidic flush of pleasure of a twisted lemon peel, of lemon seeping into a cut you didn't know you had. The rooms of these poems, as G'Sell writes, 'Seek out pleasure until pleasure itself becomes sad...'
— Emily Bludsworth de Barrios

I encountered a voice incisive and clever and was reminded of an English word borrowed from French: *chatoyant*, meaning: having a luster like that of a cat's eye at night. The verse deepens to reveal prisms and multichromatic facets. The many loanwords English adopts from French shimmer with the significance of duality. Formally fine-tuned, often in couplets, G'Sell's clean lines are time and again turned to evoke surprise. Full focus falls on each word—words marked by intently stinging, lush beauty.
— Mary-Alice Daniel

Think of these filaments as a fine and unrelenting rain (a summer rain, a 'lower-cased' rain) falling slantwise against the bare shoulders of a woman as she breezes through the city, and you trailing just behind, picking up coins and wrappers or whatever treasures she happens to drop from her open palms. Though she continuously charms and then eludes you, still with a wink she might suddenly turn on her heel to assure you—there is indeed 'no need to touch in order to grasp' her.
— Stella Corso

PRAISE for Eileen G'Sell

These poems are brilliant. I mean, they truly are. They have an eye for the most beautiful leaf on a tree. There isn't a boring poem in the lot. There really isn't. And each of these poems wants to be read, and I feel rewarded when I plop down into them. They know how to tell a joke, they know how to tell a story without getting buried by the story. The prose poems, especially, are brilliant. They are monologues more than stories, but they don't have a stage—I mean, they don't have a clear mission for which to hold your attention. What they do is meander in and around some brilliant truths, the big big truths—nothing solid saves—love and death and pain and joy, but all with the lightness of an accident. These poems listen to the brightest spots of a conversation, and then tighten the brightness into a perfect set of sentences, or arrange the brightness onto a string, like a string of bulbs sort of thing. The prose poems here are like a string of bulbs. Different colored bulbs. Sometimes a little blip of Dottie Lasky, but maybe a bigger blip of Rachel Glaser, whose poems I love. These poems are made of all new all fresh sentences. You are the expert of sentences. Dr. Sentence. You should be a judge, because you're good at sentences. I've been sentenced.
— Zachary Schomburg

I don't know where to begin praising Eileen G'Sell's *Life After Rugby*, and so I'll begin outside it, and say it reads like a culmination of much American poetry of the last 20 years ('every America / making its mark'), though this never seems to weigh it down, though it so often seems light, effortless even, though it is always perfectly itself. At the end of the book, G'Sell writes, 'I have made light of many things / and that's why we can see in here,' and when I read those lines for the first time, suddenly I did see: *Life After Rugby* is a fully realized, and therefore rare, debut, and a lifetime of a book.
— Shane McCrae

I take deep pleasure in these poems, wishing to park in front of them—sexy and larger than life as they are—with my feet up and a big bowl of popcorn. In a collection peppered with odes to films and stars, an elegy for Whitney Houston, and more than a few surprises, Eileen G'Sell gives us more than a little 'history, hilarity, the strewn blooms of rhyme.' Settle in, my friends. You are in for a treat.
— D. A. Powell

I wish I could wear the poems in G'Sell's gorgeous debut like armor because I swear they are made out of silk and guts and mischief and happiness and hope and jokes and heartbreak and patch and rasp and ruin and wink and stray and stay and 'millions of suns' and thin strange roads and holes and strong wings. They are as down to earth as they are untouchable. With these poems on, I think we might get out of here alive.
— Sabrina Orah Mark

Here, the play of language and what might be 'made light of' leads to authentic truth and beauty under other names and in other forms. We find it in pop culture, the colloquial, the reality of lives lived, and the surreal and transcendent inside the quotidian. These poems make us look and listen, then elicit double takes, as any given line might be one 'that lifts her word for skirt from the page'.
— Dora Malech

There's an inclusive, Whitmanesque charm to *Life After Rugby*, as if we're being led by a keen observer through a cosmos of human beauty and complexity... heterogeneity of character, tone, and perspective is the norm, the irreducible and insoluble fact of our shared existence.

— Tom Simpson, *The Kenyon Review*

Masterful at juxtaposition and possessing an uncanny sense of the tremulous line where agency, violence, desire, and otherness collide, G'Sell's sinuous, protean poems defy, in turns, logic, reason, and gravity, while she inscribes the self and its instability in a way that shows language, mind, and landscape to be inextricably bound.

— Virginia Konchan, *Pleiades*

This collection asks that we reverse engineer a sweet cocktail of intoxicants: linguistic beauty, mischief, and seductive arrangement. Because once the swoon settles, the emotional honesty sends us again into tailspin. These poems say: It's time to face the pain. But beauty tempers hard truths.

— Christine No, *The Rumpus*

In today's feminist landscape, women writers often address having to navigate the violence of men, but in *Life After Rugby*, violence is not something that men enact on women, or that even the powerful enact upon the weak. Instead, G'Sell sees aggression as a natural energy that permeates not only the glittery world of Hollywood films, but every human interaction—from the experience of visiting a new city to falling in love.

— Arielle Bernstein, *DIAGRAM*

Life After Rugby brings together an ensemble cast of Americans—Mike Tyson, Sigourney Weaver, Clint Eastwood, Laura Ingalls, Whitney Houston—to attest to the remaining need for resilience and toughness in an age that's proving traditional notions of masculinity so destructive. It's a collection that's interested in power, in reminding readers that not all power is inherited, that Darwinian competition isn't just an excuse for cruelty but also a fact of life we have to deal with as terrestrial creatures.

— Joe Sacksteder, *Quarterly West Review*

Here is a speaker who relishes a contest, a dare, a taunt. A challenge is always worth it, G'Sell seems to say, whether that challenge is driving across the country, finding a way to make a plane ride wildly entertaining, or tracking down a 'room of Russian balloons' for a lover...The challenges almost always boil down to an admonition to be... better. Realer, funnier, tougher, truthier.

— JoAnna Novak, *Los Angeles Review of Books*

These poems are swift, smart, and eager—at times plainly written and at other times leaping through associations via sound, image, reference, and even a little wilderness...The more you sit with these poems, the more they show their multivalence as they explore the complexities of our fast-paced, media-saturated 21st century.

— Paige Webb, *The Common Reader*

CONTENTS

~3~

Francofilaments

Eileen G'Sell

Broken Sleep Books

ISBN: 978-1-916938-50-2

Cover designed by Aaron Kent

Edited by Andre Bagoo

Typeset by Aaron Kent

Broken Sleep Books Ltd
PO BOX 102
Llandysul
SA44 9BG

For Ari,
who makes life so much easier to pronounce

By one of those rhetorical tricks inherent in self-representation, this truthful portrait is, by the very excess of its sincerity, the height of artifice and seduction. It declares precisely that which it pretends not to say.

— Nathalie Léger on a photograph of Isabelle Huppert, *Exposition*

I asked Isabelle whether she was happy.
'I never ask myself, so I suppose the answer is yes.'

— Simone De Beauvoir, *The Woman Destroyed*

FLÂNEUSE

On all sides, all city long
the devil trees escort me.

Niel says, 'I am often.'
And sometimes I agree.

The escalator, sparkling
path to wherever joy is rational,

will start too high to hear
the dead, the summer birds and breeze.

Faith is just fear of being
alone, flowers notwithstanding.

I won't cry over crinoline,
but I want my money back.

~1~

BLUE (1993)

A pool, the sky, a wrapper flapping in the wind, a woolen scarf, a
rhinestone mobile, stained glass mottled on a moonlit road, the
stripe on a stray beach ball, a lost song, a last psalm, an adulterous
husband and wordless daughter, below the belly of a speeding
Saab the asphalt is muted beryl, rain in a sky outside blue walls,
a man in a sodden blue shirt escapes a suddenly empty house,
liberté, égalité, fraternité across a parking lot, swimming laps by
herself, cutting through the bucolic grounds, crossing littered
arrondissements, a lady game to jaywalk who is hypnotized
by headlights, white coat reflected in a close-up of her pupil,
bottomless against a bloodshot white, hands flipping a lighter as a
neighbor timidly knocks, a face reflected from a bare shoulder, a
ring that glints under naked bulbs, a crucifix on a clerical smock,
'I want no possessions, no memories, no friends, no lovers—
they're all traps'.

JULIETTE BINOCHE

Doe eyed stilettos, willowy
swagger, ebullience with a beveled

Edge of Democracy, Brazilian doc,
got dumped right after marvelous

things I thought I might regret, did not,
did nothing, did what one does when one

does not, does naughtily, unknots
a throat during clouds in March

on a morning a man lies sweetly,
unquietly, a man who is bad at lying

down the avenues I sauntered, the promenades
I tread, bragging about how close I was

to ghosting all the Frenchmen and Frenching
all the ghosts, to learning every

line up, ladies, this could be your last chance,
your fresh twist of fate, that soaring boulevard

of dreams too old to follow, of life too calm
to dread, a sparkling path that curls around

croissants and crépuscules, a quick *adieu*
to reason and hair too thick to comb

the lost pages dog-eared with unbearable
precision, her mouth a long, cool *j'adore*

and her heart singing darkly

The next time I come to fuck Tim, the aspens will be older,
my memories younger, a glass of Perrier winking in the light.
The light will be dappled like the soft sky that people rent
for weddings. You can buy anything with enough crayons,
discounting skies and taxis. Tim dislikes cerulean, so I disarm the
denim. I ready the chariots and write off his taxes. Fold the pages
gently, send them to the law. The last time I counted, marigolds
were legal. The first time I cameoed, no one could tell it was me.

LA VEILLE DE NOËL

He spent a hundred dollars on boulevardiers
then loaned me a pair of Army shorts.

I bled between dreams of unwashed nights
to the bells of children's hymns.

No appetite for anything but our floating
heartbeats, Ginny and I quit teaching

to be midnight bandits, tag boys
from the snow to scarlet their shirts.

'Too much tongue', the coroner said.
The time had come to eat all the chips.

I borrowed a white bikini to plunge
into St. Lawrence. Steam trailed us

up the stairs, strangers clapped in fluffy robes.

PRIX FIXE, LUNDI

Listen, I just couldn't text you back. I was rifling through a bin of panties in Paris. 'Voila!' a diligent brunette said. 'C'est bonne!' declared a blonde. I stashed a blue green number in a metal basket. I bought silly man-undies of which I'm sure you would approve. I don't mind the cigarettes, if the ceiling feels heavenly. I fully intend at eighty to smoke after any and every glass of wine. It occurs to me now that you are that glass, that pretzels taste better than they ought to. When the sun comes out, two women in hats approach with fruit in a wooden bowl. Starved lips in the gloam, you select two cherries.

ENSUITE

My ego, crane shot
western sky, shrugged off

prairies, famous men,
bored easily, abandoned

flatsheets, took a train
of thought to Nice,

smoothed a plan
for loose dessert

NOUVELLES ANNÉES

When I was on molly and Mitra was my mom, I started to feel like it all made sense. We stood, two (or three) of us, and my shoes stopped hurting. Her large eyes, dark, and kind, looked nothing like my own. Her husband, he had eyes, too, but I don't remember seeing them. I just remember knowing that Mitra was my mom, that time could be tender if I softened my grip.

QUID PRO QUO

You've been sending sweet texts, so I'm giving you a blow job.
Should this come as a surprise, just thank your SMSes: the
emoji-less charm of a dozen spelled-out 'kiss'es at the airport,
'Ma Cherie' on an inexpensive ferry down the Seine, or learning
I'm the 'girl of [your] dreams' while my Uber scolds a pedestrian.
I thought you would want to know the specific reason for this
action. I try to be reasonable. And I traffic in specifics.

LÉA SEYDOUX

Egg-shell, boy brow, gap between

the gap between a tight tuxedo and fragile
man, ball-gowned and glowering, baby

butch denim, scissor gimmick, ankles
weeping improbable joy, gaze

tilted ever elsewhere
ludic snark where

the pastries are fresh

PRIX FIXE, MARDI

Starved lips in the gloam, you select two cherries. When the sun comes out, two women approach with fruit in a wooden bowl. It's free and they beseech you to eat it. It occurs to me now that these pretzels taste better than they ought. I fully intend at eighty to smoke after any and every glass of wine. I don't mind the cigarettes, if the ceiling feels heavenly. I buy silly man-undies of which I'm sure you would approve, stash a blue green number into an awkward metal basket. 'Voila!' a diligent brunette says. 'C'est bonne!' declares a blonde. Listen, I just couldn't text you back.

MARION COTILLARD

More Annabel Lee than Lady Dior
what part of the body clasps on command

or blinks the morning after my first
mirage splashed my face in shallow sky

I was alone and not dead inside
this ocean, your favorite plot of luxury

dirt, exposition for right at the turn
at the end of the pier, a bet with the moon

that anyone can mimic a free spirit
in a flowy skirt, the least corporeal

option is what we're going to get

MORNING SEX

I didn't hear you say Charles De Gaulle and thought you meant
the mayor. It's true I held your hand like a man. Your fridge, clean
as alien spacecraft, makes me want to mess your mattress. I love
that you love the name Lina Bembe. I hate the movie she starred
in. Lie back now as I feign alarm at the things you think about
saying.

ATOMIUM RIPOSTE

Babs, who is Belgian and lives in Baltimore, recommends a
Brussels brasserie. Babs from the New York book launch, the
novel hers, the lighting magic. The book launch at which I tipsied
and someone thought I was Tavi Gevinson, the launch after which
I joined a threesome, but only half-way (girl too young). My past
stashed in a bag bought for summer and for sequins, a beautiful
man of twenty offers up a gratis glass. No matter the age, the
skyline mocks the unoffended pigeons. I'll take olives with that
elegy (and I dislike olives). And I'll take this afternoon to relish,
to repent. Who are you, historic view, to profit from my mischief?
The cathedral meets my gaze, and says, 'You are my cathedral.'

VIRGINIE EFIRA

Seek out pleasure until pleasure
itself becomes sad and slips through

cracks in the street unpaved
for years I was redundant

to myself, orange number robbed
of approximate waist, unnatural

penchant for perfect posture, flowers
dumped that could be dried

by the fire, she was running out of
options to pretend to be young

enough to redirect traffic, pedaling
north in platform heels, mane flying

behind her like a flag you could salute

~2~

WHITE (1994)

A frayed tag, a collar hugging a staid tie, the breast of a pigeon
on courthouse steps, a boxy hatchback, metro tile, dirty snow
outside a train, a toilet lid lifted to welcome vomit, smug at the
stand with Veronica Lake hair, the echo of bridal heels down
the aisle as she greets the white sky and white rice in a white
veil, magnificent teeth in a giant smile, shivering on the street,
a corduroyed crotch kneaded by a white palm, smuggled back
home in an oversized bag, a rococo statue of a milk maid in the
window, a portrait of the virgin and child in a rural Polish cabin,
staging a funeral with a stranger's corpse, climax after 24 seconds
of missionary bliss, through opera glasses, a prison cell. 'If I say
I love you, you don't understand. If I say I hate you, you don't
understand'.

AMÉLIE POULAIN

The key to the city is the city
Instamatic eyelash a skeleton

cure for the human inside
a photo booth no longer here

a flock of rouge lollies
winging a roughened clown

blind to the baby watching
a dog watching the chickens

already dead, a surge of love
of sugarplum ice cream, melon slices

a slender widow who smiles
the first and very last time

a crowd cobblestones past
the fountain absent coins and fragile

dreams, the Great Romance is never
about money or candy or bonneted children

but the wordless letter tucked under your door

BARBARA CHASE-RIBOUD

Burnished arc of a woman's hips, warmth
        of a hand braiding cord into rope,
lightness brushes depth to coax new
        mythos out of matter,

the brooch on the breast, shedding
        lashes, monoliths, our oldest
alloy, crimson dripping from part
        of the body no one

warned us about, suspended
        before an earnest crowd, caught
in the song of stringless harps, a bundle of
        'something...silver and fabulous',

silk on the wrist of the rest of the world,
        a time before Paris, Rome,
Philadelphia, before Malcolm, Mao, and
        Marian Anderson, after

Cleopatra sat ramrod on a throne, read
        Gertrude Stein for the very last time,
closed her eyes and opened her hands
        to a future void of famine

ADÈLE EXARCHOPOULOS

So many *O*s in a name
so hungry for the apocalypse

thunderstorm mouth empty
bottle of blue mascara

nightmares to verb a lack of
vanity makes her even

more attractive to men
who hate unnatural orgasms

I soprano no matter art's
rise as commerce, clever

ruse for dumbfounding
orifice of ordinary need

THE GENEROSITORS

The Generositors were like muggers, but in lieu of stealing your money they would foist great funds upon you. There you were, recycling a bottle or wrangling a terrier, and there they were, brash from an SUV, accosting you on the sidewalk. Pushed to the bricks of a store or station, you'd wonder what they would ask for. What should I try to hand over? What will I have to spread? But no sooner did thoughts assail the limbs than a package hurled at your collar: one hundred thousand Euros, organized into ten neat stacks. By the time the flash of pastel notes made shocking sense, the Generositors were gone and the promenade empty. A stab of relief, then joy, would come, then alarm at how quickly one led to the next. The French were struck with yen, the Japanese were rushed with rubles. The British were clocked with kroner; the Danes were downed with pounds. No one was attacked with US dollars because US dollars are ugly. The Generositors were aesthetes, their cufflinks white in the late day sun.

VICKY KRIEPS

What is a motif, a woman
in mourning for her own body

of work impresses
the queen, a single

mother of no invention beyond
the invention of the mother

something we can all be proud of
ourselves, grit in the face

of reason, delight a bike
of rusted doubt, neon lights

an empty stage, a dog
dragging a yellow leash en route

to a mother of ankles, tight
adventures in leather

books line the lobby the colour
of sea floor, naked theory

of womanly everything
you thought you knew

escapism, however tenuous, proves
the only recourse to agency

NOONERS

Let me be your Elizabeth Warren. Your wristwatch glints (but I
don't watch watches). My 'escort' body adores the conceptual art
you made and hung over the bed. I love the idea of you (alone)
with pink construction paper, of you with heavy duty scissors
doing anything with a shred of rage. Your fantasy of a midday
round-armed-sofa-bound bukkake? Soooo autumn 2012. I will
always be angrier than you could guess. I will always know
what time it is. Resplendent as words you can't possibly mean,
redundant as sex in your native tongue, it makes sense I'm the one
who would mouth the hour's instructions, who would show you
how perfectly to pronounce the word 'boss'.

CÉLINE SCIAMMA

You gave me breathing lessons I thought
I didn't need, a space and time

to velvet forests, liquid crystal
displays of taste where time

is a level of depth to image, rumble
like we could all float away from

the hum of home, the rhythm of teeth
punctiliously brushed, the scratch of pencil

on old loose leaf, two who sister ponytail
bramble, oak tree forts of billowing

girls, you didn't invent my sadness, you
stained its satin in just the right way

CLOSE (2022)

Two boys sprint through a pink field, elbows and knees spearing the air.

Two boys through a field of knees, the air pinking their elbows.

Two boys field the pink air, sprinting past elbowed knees.

Two boys spear the pink, fielding knees, air, and elbows.

Two boys knee the field air, sprinting through the pink.

Two boys elbow the air, sprint through spears.

Two boys air the elbow field.

Two boys pink the air.

LES PARAPLUIES DE CHERBOURG (1964)

the rain lower-cased when i was barely
grown, i developed a penchant for kind

mechanics, the kind who sing in open
rooms that smell of egalitarianism,

another term for love beyond that
permitted among authorities better

dressed for disaster than today
is the day i tried and failed to visit

Agnès Varda's grave, a kiss-stained
stone shared with Demy, who did not

die of cancer, she revealed four years
after the rainy day i watched Catherine

on the big screen, picked a coin
from a cedar box my sister gave me

from a thankless land pages away from
a pleated skirt, crown contrived of paper gold,

honest memory to go on living
when dying was not enough

FACTS ARE FACTS

I'm glad I didn't off myself because I got a ticket to Isabelle
Huppert. Same-day, fifteen Euros, a ninety-minute monologue
from Mary, Queen of Scots. I've always liked dark spaces, benches
shared with foreign strangers. I dislike dad jokes and too many
throw pillows, flat screen televisions in soft-lit bars. Isabelle
wound herself white on white, her corset coughing up Stuart red.
Adieu, ma mère. Adieu, la France. I understood little and loved it
all, thought that was how to live my life. *Mes mains, mes amis*, are
stronger than they look. My father bequeathed a deadly grip.

LAURE CALAMY

Wanting to be a person easy
to forgive, a shoe worn out

to difficult parties hosted in
rooms with views of shoes

moving shoes others choose
to step on someone slower, taller

than speech from the metro
mouth a small apology

to anyone fluffing their pillows
reading the news, the road

to success is paved with shoes
escorting leather ankles, shoes

wanted for heavy roads, a dog-eat-dog
world can make anyone a bitch

LA RÈGLE DU JEU (1939)

Complicit in their follies, we are shocked at their extremes, the
frog-guarded greenhouse at the edge of war, the perspiration
on André's brow, the circles rimming Christine's eyes, the
paisley scarf with which Robert blots his face below the spots on
Geneviève's chapeau, the servants folding tablecloths, tossing
pillow-cases, beating trees with sticks to rouse the rabbits the
rich will eat, the polka-dotted tie of an indigent poacher whose
traps are just as quick as his hands, the portly hanger-on to the old
haute monde who also directs the movie, knowing lawless wealth
makes a farce of us all

MAI 68

I taught *Tout va Bien* in a Missouri
prison, the subtitles missing, students

filled in the blanks with 'Merci beau coup',
'Au revoir', 'Let them eat cake', the workers

work, the bourgeois bourgeois
a potato tower set on fire, sixteen

workers whip the clapperboard,
potato the foreground, magic-marker blood

on cotton aprons, in the country there is
countryside, social theatre, supermarket chains of

torn receipts, certified love, the free market
and free produce we pretend to love and shut

our mouths, 'Be realistic, demand the impossible,'
Jane Fonda in her *Klute* 'do the star

to make the movie happen, hurried cheques
in manly hands the joke of revolution

CLAIRE DENIS

Sex with a revolutionary does not make
                one revolutionary. Power is never just
power, she says, I don't want to be a nurse

or doctor, just an observer, flat cokes
                and slow fans and hair splayed
formidable, a penchant for developing

countries does not make one an expert,
                eros via erasure, the bedding
and shedding of white material via

Costa Rica, Nicaragua, Cameroon,
                Djibouti, interchangeable as
neutral shapewear, cool as patrician

table manners, filial cheeks and freckled duty,
                a hatless riposte on a speeding bike
hauling baskets of coffee berries,

a cultivated ignorance (or is it guilt),
                cold as the petri dish she
straddles, stuns, and smirks at the world

TINA TURNER IN PARIS

No need to touch in order to grasp
fifty and floating off the Eiffel

muse to Alaïa, Lindbergh, body of
music three decades strong, gold

beaded swagger, velvet strut, eye full
of bicep flexed for the sky

overcast and underslept, muse to
her own indefatigable self, hemmed

in tight cotton, brow to the sun,
she swapped her passport for another

country that loved her better, not
because it understood her

but because it didn't try to
exhaust the ways a woman can

be touched in order to touch
her country, of course, has all but forgot

AVANT MONTREAL

In the parking lot of a post office closed in Detroit, the man I
thought I loved asked me why I was crying. Happiness isn't a
choice, I said, considering the plaza. I will never be the minimalist
you want me to be, that you so extravagantly think that you are.
A dead line, a bad path, a too-big coat in an ancient Saab. I have
always preferred potatoes to pathology, especially fried into sticks
of starch. Why not drown in salt, fat, a slow hello to sidewalks?
Heaven is not defeat, Detroit, your newly defanged beautiful pet.
It is a poster of perroquettes tacked to the wall, a stained Moka
pot gurgling softly, the sound of church bells from a giant church
and the children who learn on its playground, the sounds of
children like clever birds that land on my wrists to rest.

CHARLOTTE GAINSBOURG

White flag at half mast, wiry
brain in mother's boots,

you lost your cat in Brooklyn,
and my friend read the flyer.

Lemon dream, tight bride, sinew
on a wooded night, how long

can the looming cirrus clouds
bitter sky without us? We who

walk on the shoulder, and
shoulder the road, till full

and absent-minded, we who
fill the margins with ridiculous

precision, who know exactly who
we are, and still give over, in

~3~

RED (1994)

Postage stamps, a leather chair, *Economist* masthead, telephone
cables, alarm clock, a gleaming Jeep, twin cherries on a yogurt
label that becomes a slot machine, the blood of a dog run over
on the road, the cover of a Droit *pénal général* textbook, another
doe-eyed pensive brunette, the floor of her ballet studio where
she arches her back and guzzles a giant bottle of water, an animal
heaved into a tiny car and rushed to the residence listed on its
collar, an elderly recluse who eavesdrops, face in the glass of a
framed painting of a historic scene, a cheerful trip on a gloomy
catwalk, a storm that hits the English Channel, luxury ferry
sent to sea floor, 'People aren't bad . . . they may just be weak
sometimes.'

FIRE AT THE DOLL FACTORY

Celluloid's cheaper than porcelain
said a fragile man in a sturdy suit

the water around his shaking knees
I knew I'd never seen before

the flood of 1910, Paris swaddled
itself in silk, tremulous gleams

from bobbing eyes, a blinking line
in a stream of clarity

one ought not swim with painted
brows, said he who lifted me

over the void that once had been
our moonlit street women

watched in crimson gloves, my hips
milk beneath my skirts, it is too late

to begin living if one has already started to die

AGNÈS VARDA

She didn't think it was difficult to live
   her life, flute-filled credits, half-
bleached bowl cut and Susan Sontag

asking pointed questions in 1969
   one of the few to gain approval
to visit Panther headquarters,

a devotion to cats and heart-shaped
   everything, 'nothing is trite... with empathy
and love', a busker swallowing multiple

frogs, a woman lying blank on a beach
   with a Bible over her bosom,
eccentric genius, patron saint of

potatoes and unconventional thinking,
   who outlived Truffaut but not Godard
who fled to the cranky countryside

CANCER

I hugged a girl much skinnier than me—who was not supposed to be skinny. I lit candles in European cathedrals, plus one in Montreal. I bought her earrings that, truthfully, I wanted to buy myself. I got on my knees and talked to a God I did not believe in. I thought about her, how the earrings would look better on her than me. I wanted to see them glisten. I wanted to see her gleam. And I know, Randall, that you want peace. But I want conflagration. I want to topple every votive glass lining Notre-Dame. You mow the lawn at seven am while I imagine arson. You hand me a foiled mac-n-cheese and twelve-ounce Canada Dry. I didn't know your daughter well, but I hear a choir singing. The mezzos crescendo: *Let the motherfucker burn.*

JULIA DUCOURNAU

If you've ever wanted to fuck a firetruck
or feast on a friend, ask which

is more natural, the pulsing under
the hood or beneath a woman's navel,

a dipstick glistens, a body bleeding
motor oil belches life, tremulous purr

of rubber on pavement, the urge
to claw a V8 thrum, caliginous belly,

stick shift to slush box,
horror or compassion

is always combustible

JEAN SEBERG

I don't remember a storm
in the story but thunder

in the cut. A Breton
boat-necked possibility,

pregnant on the street.
There were other scenes,

from other films, but few
who cared to listen,

all mafia and mascarpone
spread thin against the Seine.

I've gone fugitive too,
my ambition in life

to become immortal,
then suddenly and quietly die.

PARC LAHAIE

When you wish to forget, but cannot,
your dog runs with you in the rain. You have
nowhere to go but a woman's flat

you have rented in a city. The woman,
a dear and beautiful friend, is not just
a woman, but you are just

a woman tonight, a woman rushing
home in the rain. 'I should have ordered
you both a car', a man and could-be

father texts, 'instead of watching you
leave in the rain.' You've run in worse places,
and in worse shoes, but now,

you're running off with your dog,
running quietly in the rain. He is old,
but keeps up. You two have always been

good at running. Your dog is tall, smart,
good, and fast, his legs warm
with summer rain.

CLAIR DE LUNE

I've been alive a long time, a tongued lime
in August, a soft rhyme floating

down the tenth arrondissement. I am
a Fontainebleau moth, white as death,

a sunlit lawn of untouched grass, the dark
horse by a split tree who never returns

your focus, or, if he does, turns at once
to the sound of bells a forest away

from a town he will never visit,
knowing full well that neither will you.

MADAME HYDE (2017)

If a character is essential
you must pay attention

to what they are and how
they change the thankless air

sparks all day a new life
story that takes too long

to dread the essential work
of pages, lawless incalescence,

if a character is essential
lighting strikes you

must show who she is
till she's nobody else

JOSEPHINE BAKER

The home she had in my hometown has been gone for ninety years.
No plaque, no statue, just a sidewalk star five miles away.
The home she had was other people's home. 5,000 buildings razed.
In an interview for the *Post-Dispatch*, she said 2632 Bernard St.
was 'obliterated for a highway'. It was not obliterated for a highway.
The highway was erected when she was shaking banana feathers at
Casino de Paris, getting rich and famous being cheeky and brilliant.
2632 Bernard was razed because St. Louis leaders wanted to take
out the largest Black community in the city, the fourth biggest city
in the US. She did not come back to her home because it was not
her home. Her new home was a dream. Real homes always are.

CHÂTEAU POTENSAC, MEDOC, 1975

My God-bless-yous aren't empty, but
        these woods are unkind. The bottle
kept on its own in the back wasn't
        special at all, it turns out. How I'd love

to say that of you, to say that of anyone
        who pelted me with the virtues
of beauty, the vitriol of besting the one
        claimed once beloved. I let the bad ones in

so brilliantly the blackbirds circled
        decades a week. I let myself down
from the tallest tree. I downed the good
        that smelt of soil, of giving over, in.

Even my absolutions finish hard, if this be
        absolution. My tongue stained by gnarled
verbs, every sham thing you labeled
        treasure, I treasured.

ISABELLE HUPPERT

Vengeance is as dignified

an option as any, less lightning
than thunder, less timbre

than quake. Collared encore,
blank applause, trains stalled

for towns at a time. What good can
come of bad handsomes? What god

would hum through a hurricane?

APRÈS LE D&C

When I braved the wind for unnamed fruit, the sea
and trees for shallow depths, the answer clung
to my inner thighs as I turned to building an empire.
I was sad to be done and glad to be scraped,
and my books remained unopened. The first was
on the art of recklessness, the next on neorealism.
Or rather, "After Neorealism." I admit to know
no difference. Do you see how they lie so still,
so new, as cicadas die downstairs of lust?

As I wait here for you, bitter and perfect.
As I tell you to stay, and do what you want.

NOTES

The epigraph excerpts from Nathalie Léger's *Exposition*, translated by Amanda DeMarco, and published by the Dorothy Project, St. Louis, in 2020; as well as Simone De Beauvoir's *The Woman Destroyed*, translated by Patrick O'Brian, and published by Pantheon Books, New York, in 1969. 'Tina Turner in Paris, 1989', 'Vicky Krieps', 'Fire at the Doll Factory', and '*Madame Hyde* (2017)' excerpt or reshape short phrases from *Exposition*.

The following poems excerpt content from interviews I conducted with French or French-speaking actors and filmmakers from 2018–23:

'Juliette Binoche': 'On Mothers, Daughters, and "The Truth": A Conversation with Juliette Binoche', *Los Angeles Review of Books*, July 3, 2020.

'Céline Sciamma': 'Breathing Lessons: An Interview with Céline Sciamma', *Reverse Shot*, April 22, 2022.

'*Madame Hyde* (2017)': 'In *Mrs. Hyde* Isabelle Huppert Is a Different Kind of Dr. Jekyll', *VICE,* April 27, 2018.

The following poems repurpose snippets of prose from an array of film reviews, profiles, and essays I published in the following outlets from 2018–23:

'Marion Cotillard': 'Marion Cotillard and Charlotte Gainsbourg Spar in a Haunting Love Triangle', *Hyperallergic*, March 22, 2018.

'Virginie Efira': 'The Other Women', *Reverse Shot*, April 20, 2023.

'Céline Sciamma': 'In Praise of Small Hope: *Petite Maman* and Ambivalent Motherhood', *The Hopkins Review*, Volume 15, Number 1, Winter 2022, pp. 177–183.

'*Close* (2022)': 'Imperiled Intimacy & Lukas Dhont's *Close* (2022)', *The Hopkins Review*, Volume 16, Number 3, Summer 2023, pp. 51–55.

'Laure Calamy': 'Extraordinary Hustle: A Profile of Laure Calamy', *Los Angeles Review of Books*, February 6, 2023.

'*La Règle du Jeu* (1939)': 'Why *The Rules of the Game* Is Still Required Viewing', *Hyperallergic*, January 31, 2023.

'Claire Denis': 'Claire Denis's New Film Is Stronger on Steam Than Story', *Hyperallergic*, November 1, 2022

'On *Two Sides of the Blade*: Denis, Binoche, and Fraught (White) Femininity', *The Hopkins Review*, Volume 15, Number 3, Summer 2022, pp. 123-126

'Juliette Binoche Offers a Tantalizing Performance in Her Two Latest Films', *Hyperallergic*, May 24, 2019

'Walking Tall: Claire Denis's *White Material*', *Reverse Shot*, December 15, 2023.

'Barbara Chase-Riboud': 'Barbara Chase-Riboud Breathes Life into Bronze', *Hyperallergic*, January 22, 2023.

'Julia Ducournau': 'The Automotive-Erotic Body Horror of *Titane*', *Hyperallergic*, November 4, 2021;

'*Titane* Takes Body Horror into Glorious, Gender-Bending Overdrive', *Riverfront Times*, October 20, 2021.

'Agnès Varda': 'The Eccentric Genius of Agnès Varda', *Hyperallergic*, February 8, 2020.

'Three Colors Trilogy': 'Reflections on Brilliance: Krzysztof Kieślowski's Three Colors Trilogy', *The Hopkins Review*, Volume 15, Number 4, Fall 2022, pp. 178–187.

ACKNOWLEDGMENTS

Like poems themselves, some books take years to finish, while others suddenly appear all but fully formed. This book is a bit of both, and I thank the brilliant Virginia Konchan for heartily encouraging me to turn a former chapbook into what I like to call a 'feature length' collection of poetry. I also thank JoAnna Novak and Nathaniel Rosenthalis, whose faith in the virtues of aesthetic pleasure proved an abiding source of confidence as I wrote these poems, and whose speedy feedback helped me finalize the original manuscript. I am also indebted to the magazine and journal editors who have nurtured my voice as a film critic, without whom many these poems would never have gestated: Erin Keane, Annie Berke, Chloe Lizotte, Michael Koresky, Dora Malech, Chad Perman, and Natalie Haddad. I am also grateful to the those at Cinetic Media, Oscilloscope, and Music Box Films who made me aware of so many recent Francophone films, including Sophie Gluck, Rachel Allen, Kaitlyn Cummings, Julie Chappell, Emilie Spiegel, and Charlie Olsky. Without their efforts, I never would have had the opportunity to interview so many luminous filmmakers and screen actors.

Thanks to the Center for the Humanities at Washington University in St. Louis for providing a quiet, sunlit space to work on this manuscript.

Finally, I thank the editors at the journals and literary magazines in which the following poems were published, sometimes under an alternative title

'Après le D&C'	*Fence*
'Isabelle Huppert'	*Fence*
'64 Ct Glory Box'	*DIAGRAM*
'Juliette Binoche'	*DIAGRAM*
'Morning Sex'	*LIT*
'Château Potensac, Medoc, 1975'	*Oversound*
'Nouvelles Années'	*Matter*
'Facts Are Facts'	*Matter*
'Jean Seberg'	*Air / Light*
'Flâneuse'	*Air / Light*
'Atomium Riposte'	*Berlin Lit*
'Prix Fixe, Lundi'	*Tammy*
'Prix Fixe, Mardi'	*Tammy*
'La Veille de Noël'	*Politics/Letters*
'Nooners'	*Tupelo Quarterly*
'Parc Lahaie'	*Berlin Lit*

EXPOSE TON MALAISE

www.ingramcontent.com/pod-product-compliance
Lightning Source LLC
Chambersburg PA
CBHW020216090426
42734CB00008B/1100